EMPOWERING TRUTH

Real Stories About Overcoming
Domestic Violence & Abuse

EMPOWERING TRUTH

Real Stories About Overcoming Domestic Violence & Abuse

TINA R. McCREA

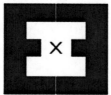

EXPECTED END

ENTERTAINMENT

Atlanta, GA

PRAISE FOR EMPOWERING TRUTH

"As a licensed clinical therapist with a background in Post-Traumatic Stress Disorder, having access to books like *Empowering Truth: Real Stories About Overcoming Domestic Violence & Abuse* provides additional resources to help my clients who have experienced the impact of trauma as a result of domestic violence."

Sharise M. Nance, LCSW, CCTP, author of Vitamin C: The Healing Workbook

"It was difficult to relive my mother's physical and emotional abuse by my father, and her eventual death at 37. But writing about it released a lot of the pain, anger, and sorrow that followed me for years. *Empowering Truth: Real Stories About Overcoming Domestic Violence & Abuse* brings that same healing power and shows you what is on the other side of going through the furnaces of Hell. I recommend it as a constant companion for your daily walk."

James E. McMillan, author of *Freedom's Challenge: Asking Life's Difficult Questions, Answers to Overcome Them*, and *How to Get Anything Paid For*

"Tina has pulled back the shades on an ugly epidemic and has allowed light to come in for the freedom of many.

Dr. D'Ann Johnson, author of Notes From My Bible. Devotional and Executive Pastor of New Covenant Christian Ministries

"All we can say is, wow! This book is the equivalent of an emotional and spiritual underground railroad. This book will serve as a declaration of independence in regards to coming out of abuse. Come aboard for the ride of your life."

Apostle Phil & Pastor Mia Huff

MORE PRAISE FOR EMPOWERING TRUTH

"What a spirited story of how the simplicity of intimacy can digress into aggression & then violence. *Empowering Truth: Real Stories About Overcoming Domestic Violence & Abuse* clearly unfolds the traumatic nightmare of what is felt, experienced as a victim of domestic violence. As a Survivor who has shared my journey from victim to victor I understand but commend Author Tina McCrea for having the courage to share her story as well. Share a story, save a life."
Survivor and Author Sheila B., founder of the domestic violence organization No Longer the Face Foundation

"Empowering Truth is truly a story of redemption. It is a must read for any woman struggling to make a bad situation better. Empowering Truth provides the wisdom to break free and stay free, enabling us to live a God-ordained life. Domestic violence is a hidden virus in the church. Empowering Truth takes the lid off the hidden secrets that are destroying the credibility of the family."
Prophet Alexis Alexander

Published by Expected End Entertainment/EX3 Books
info@EX3Books.com * www.EX3Books.com
ISBN-10: 0-9961722-9-7
ISBN-13: 978-0-9961722-9-5
Printed in the United States of America

DEDICATION

I dedicate this book to every woman who has found herself in this *"seemingly"* place of no return. You may feel as if you're stuck at a dead-end with no way out or your back is up against the wall. You may even feel as if you do not have anywhere to go or anyone to confide in. If this is you or you know someone who is in this situation, keep reading! This book is not a fictional story; it is factual! I pray that the Word of God and the testimonies speak to you. I pray that you are compelled to move forward through the victory outlined in my personal story. Once you break free, stay free and be free, then pay it forward and share your story so that someone else can be empowered to be free.

I also want to dedicate this book to my Auntie Fuzzy. The loss of your life was not in vain. You changed my destiny and the destiny of many.

CONTENTS

ACKNOWLEDGEMENTS

My heartfelt thanks to:

- ❖ My husband Apostle Gary L. McCrea, who watched my life from a distance go through shameful situations and abandonment. Yet you saw me through the eyes of Jesus Christ's love. Thank you honey for loving me and for being the godly and faithful husband and father to our child you promised to be for 17 years. I love you.

- ❖ My daughter Gina McCrea for sharing me unselfishly from your infancy with so many hurting people that I spend time listening to, coaching, and praying through their pit of pain into the presence of God.

- ❖ My spiritual daughter, prayer partner and my Ruth, Evangelist Tashara N. Luster for selecting me to be your mentor at a time when I didn't even know where my life was heading. I knew it was only going to get better in the hand of the Holy One. Thank you for allowing me to be transparent and for holding me accountable to be true to my calling for over 16 years of our life journey together.

- ❖ My cousin and little-big brother Dwayne Metcalf who has encouraged me and helped me overcome fear of failure as well as the fear of success by feeding my own words back to me and calling me from your death bed to tell me what the Lord said about me, my marriage, and my ministry.

❖ My baby brother and best friend Richard E. Winston, who walked with me through some of the darkest days of my life as a roommate in that abusive marriage and during my transition into freedom. Thank you for never losing respect for your big sister. Thank you for being my intercessor as I walked out of darkness into God's marvelous light. You are my witness that what I have written is 100% true because you saw it up close and personal, yet, you are serving faithfully by my side in ministry to this day. After all that we've seen and been through, we *ain't* scared of the devil! I love you my friend.

❖ Bishop Alicia Perry, for the many hours you spent praying me through and taking me through a life-to-life training as a mother that shaped my spiritual growth, character, and destiny for 18 years. I will forever praise God for your life and ministry.

❖ Dr. D'Ann Johnson that asked the pointed question in your sermon, "Where are the Naomi's?" Thank you for reminding me through mentoring that there are more Ruths that need what I have because "what's in the cup is for me but what pours out into the saucer is the Overflow from the Holy Spirit."

❖ Dr. Gayle Rogers for apostolic coaching that empowered and challenged me to look into the subconscious mind, invite the set apart Spirit of

God into the corridors of my mind to demolish strongholds that were keeping me from experiencing wholeness in marriage, motherhood, and ministry.

❖ Samuel Sheffield for your transformational life coaching that prepared me for the unveiling of my Jubilee and freedom to BE me.

❖ My Mom, Barbara J. Metcalf, who endured hardship, endured the pain of so many losses and showing me that we truly can be more than conquerors through Christ Jesus who loves us.

❖ Prophet Cynthia Rawles, Destined2Inspire Ministries, for listening, praying and inspiring me as you coached me through the writing process. We never know who is waiting on the other side of our obedience. I thank God for you being there.

My faithful friends, intercessors, and sisters who had the courage to share the birthing of this vision by telling their stories so that others can experience the same breakthrough from pain to praise.

TINA R. McCREA

FOREWORD
DR. GAYLE ROGERS

When domestic violence invades the Body of Christ, I believe that's one of the ways God attempts to get our attention. As He unveils truth in the midst of where we worship it's time to deal with the pain and the hurt directly from the pulpit. This is a subject that many leaders have not touched upon, many simply from fear of reprisals. Yet the enemy has captured and ensnared the daughters of God since early times -- oppressing, harassing, and abusing oftentimes, in the name of Jesus! Somewhere men have been deceived into believing a man has a right to control and abuse their women/wives and in many cases even their children. And somehow many women have believed that lie, or been so frightened for their lives or the lives of their loved ones that they didn't know what to do except remain captured in the abusive relationship. Many women have gone to their leaders in their church homes, simply to be told they must love "and obey" their husbands and trust God to fix the situation.

Unfortunately, many women believe they deserve to be mistreated, or worse yet, they don't understand mistreatment, therefore believe this is the way relationships are supposed to be. Tina's riveting account of living in a hellish relationship depicts otherwise. I hope as you read her story you will realize where you are in your own relationship. Though I've not experienced what Tina describes in her abusive marriage, I was a victim, living the first five years on this earth witnessing my parents fight each other. That constitutes abuse as well. I have been working with abused women and children for more than 30 years, and I can tell you it isn't easy pulling them out of these relationships. But once they come to understand their abuse, get beyond their fear, and take control of their lives, they then recognize their significance, thinking beyond their circumstances and simply wanting to be whole in order to help others *break free*.

Guarding one's heart and identity is tantamount to embracing this freedom. Authentic identity is often difficult to discover when one has been in bondage for decades. But as we look at the women who have paved the path to freedom, we all must be willing to embrace who we've been designed to be in order to maintain this path for the freedom of those young women coming behind us. Maya Angelou says it best: "I'm a woman Phenomenally. Phenomenal woman, That's me."

I applaud Pastor Tina. I applaud her transparency – her ability to tell her story of pain and woundedness; the emotional, mental, and physical trauma she endured; the fear, shame, and humiliation she felt to help other women become who God has called them to BE!

INTRODUCTION

As you journey through this book, you will discover that witnessing domestic violence, whether it's the first time or several times, is not a guarantee that you will not experience domestic violence in your own life. If this already describes your situation, DON'T PUT THIS BOOK DOWN, even if you're ashamed to admit that you've fallen into this trap. There is a way out for you and your shame will be exchanged for a crown of glory!

Maybe you are a person who has witnessed domestic violence and you've said to yourself, "There's no way I would ever be married and allow that to happen to me! There's no way I would allow someone to speak to me that way! There's no way I would allow someone to treat me that way! There's no way!" As you read this book, check your mindset and behaviors in your current relationship and make certain it is not actually happening to you right now.

This book opens up a dialogue for real freedom and truth. This is a life-changing story that will take you to the next level and teach you how to come out of domestic violence and abuse and never to return again! For some, it may be your saving grace! Don't get it twisted, this sickness crosses every race, gender and nationality. Many walk around with absolutely evidence of abuse and others walk around with the "that won't happen to me" attitude. Unless we can be transparent, educated, and informed, the truth will remain hidden and many more victims will suffer.

Here I was, a young lady who loved Jesus. I was filled with the Holy Spirit and speaking in tongues. I knew God's word but that didn't seem to keep me from being attracted to this type of person. Could this be the dilemma that I faced and so many others face today? Although I was confessing to be a regenerated believer in the Lord Jesus Christ, I was still living a carnal lifestyle, which is defined as a lifestyle of the flesh, denoting mere human nature, the earthly nature of man apart from divine influence, and therefore prone to sin and opposed to God.

I'm challenging some of you right here and right now. If you have stepped over into a place of carnality instead of a consecrated life, you are opening a door that leads to vulnerability and danger. Satan will attempt to stop your personal and spiritual growth and cut off your opportunity to make a difference in the lives of others. If this is the case for you, be encouraged! God can and will turn it around if you allow Him to help you.

In this book, I'm being transparent with you because I want you to see the pattern of gradually being overtaken with evil. According to the Merriam Webster's Online Dictionary, the definition of Insidious is - causing harm in a way that is gradual or not easily noticed, having a gradual and cumulative effect. a: awaiting a chance to entrap: treacherous; b: harmful but enticing: seductive (insidious drugs). Think for a moment. I've described the seduction then the gradual feeling of entrapment that unnoticeably cumulates into treacherous treatment. Sound familiar? This is REAL! How did this happen to me? Keep reading!

CHAPTER 1
SHE STAYED TOO LONG

My auntie was a very lively lady. She was somebody that I admired as a little girl because she was skinny like me but she made being skinny seem sexy. She dressed in the latest fashions, modeled professionally and drove a red convertible with the name plate "Fuzzy" in the front. Everywhere she went, men would holler out, "Hey Fuzzy!" I remember my precious auntie smiling all of the time, yet in quiet moments she would cry and sing sad love songs over and over again.

One summer day, my Auntie Fuzzy and other family members were visiting our house. We were sitting on the porch enjoying laughs and great conversation when suddenly three men came walking around the corner with blankets and large towels that covered shotguns. The men walked with determination in their eyes and fury in their steps, acting as though they were the only ones in the entire world. Whipping the blankets back like they were capes, they started blasting the shotguns and yelling profanity into our neighbor's house. We jumped up and ran frantically into the house, each person taking a window to peek out of as shots rang and rang for what seemed like thirty minutes. Auntie Fuzzy grabbed her chest and said, "Whew! I just had a feeling that I was going to die by being shot in the chest." My mother got very upset and scolded her right away for saying such a thing. You see Auntie Fuzzy was my mother's best friend. Everyone got quiet as if we had paused for her death or something.

After things calmed down, everyone was asking what would make these men commit such a horrible act. Two days prior to the shooting, one of my neighbor's sons caught a man fighting his mother. The son and his Doberman Pinscher chased the man out of the house, across the street and into the yard next door. At the same time, he pulled out a pistol and started shooting at the man. I still remember the sound of that pistol popping like a fire cracker. Later that night, the man returned the

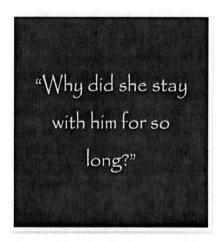

"Why did she stay with him for so long?"

neighbor's house and ended up dead. The mother killed him! I remember seeing the crime scene van in front of our house. I was so afraid that I called my uncle to come over and stay with us while my mother and father were at work. We watched as they carried the body to the van. It was my first encounter with domestic violence. The newspapers documented the man's death as the removal of a menace to society. Needless to say, his brothers sought revenge on that summer day and shot up her home in broad daylight. Fortunately, nobody was killed this time.

School had started and people were beginning to forget the horrible summer night when our neighbor killed somebody on her front porch. My cousins, my brother and I were excited about school. The three of them attended the same middle school but the rest of us were bused to different schools far from home. One day, my cousins and my brother missed their bus and decided to walk back home. For some reason, on this particular day, my brother decided to go home instead of following my cousins to their house, as he normally would. When my cousins got home, Auntie Fuzzy was there laying around and listening to those sad love songs. Her new boyfriend was there. I will call Mr. Darkness because he a scary looking man with very dark features. He came to the door with another strange man. Mr. Darkness always made me nervous but I didn't know why. My cousins heard him demanding money from my auntie while she pleaded with the men not to hurt her.

Showing no mercy or regard for her small children, the evil men shot her in the face and stomach with a shotgun, blowing off part of her head, blasting out all of internal organs. My cousins hid in the bathroom until they heard them leave. They found their mother with one hand dangling in the air until she died.

Many nights I would cry on my pillow asking God, "Why didn't my beloved auntie press charges the first time he hit her or the time when she had to jump out of a moving car to get away from him in fear for her life? Why didn't she leave Mr. Darkness when he threatened her life over and over again? Why didn't she remember what happened that summer day in our neighborhood? Why didn't someone save my auntie?"

CHAPTER 2
THE CYCLE CONTINUED IN ME

"Our greatest weakness lies in giving up. The most certain way to succeed is always to try just one more time." Thomas Edison

Eleven years after Auntie Fuzzy was killed, I found myself in a similar abusive situation. How could this be? I remember saying to myself, it would never happen to me! A simple trip to Atlanta to hang out with a friend would soon turn into a serious relationship with a man nearly 20 years older. He was a muscular man who was charming, slick and cool. He had a "bad boy" personality and for some reason I found that attractive. Ironically, he initially was not interested in me because he said that I was not holy enough for him. He told me that he was a Christian and a praying man and he assumed I wasn't. After the put downs, which were red flags of verbal abuse, he began making advances towards me. He even offered me a key to his place to come visit whenever I wanted. I thought that was noble and nice and took him up on it. I started visiting him from time-to-time and he would visit me as well. Eventually, these visits would turn into intimate and sexual encounters.

He soon began making disgraceful impulses and demands. They became increasingly prevalent in my life. I saw a look in his eyes the first day he saw me pull up in my luxury car to my apartment. Those eyes said, "Cha-Ching!" but I ignored it and assumed it was the fact that he was excited to see me. He asked me to move to Georgia and live with him. However, as a Christian lady, I initially protested and said I could not without getting married first. This conversation took place in June and we were married in August of the same year. That's where my Story began. I never realized that he was serious until it was too late. I just thought it was a put on, sort of like George Jefferson. Little did I know, he was very serious. I said to myself, "He would never do anything to harm me, even if he is kind of edgy."

I remember the flash of the photography at my wedding when I heard the Lord speak to me and say, "I am going to use this marriage as an example for the church." Immediately, I thought this meant that we were going to be rich and blessed. On the outside, it appeared that way. Even family members would say, "You all are living the life!"

The drama began the first month of our marriage. Women would call constantly and whenever I answered the phone they would hang up. I told myself it was just because he was a hair stylist and his clients may have thought they had the wrong number. This was just an excuse I had created in my own mind. He started becoming agitated when his income began to dry up. It went from $1,000 per week to $300 per week to $100 per week. I wondered why. A few months later, I noticed this lady slowly driving by the house and staring at me. She would wave and I would wave back. Finally, I asked about her? He told me that it was his ex-wife who had left him to join a cult. He spoke about how controlling the pastor and ministry was and how they put him out of the church and she insisted on staying. I thought, "How horrible that must have been and how could she." I became paranoid as she continued to drive by often. One day we were at the grocery store and ran into her and one of her church members. The guy started yelling at us in and telling us that we were going to hell. I was shaking and it reinforced in my mind that this lady actually was a part of a cult because no real Christian would act that way. I was so afraid that I would jump when the newspaper person threw a paper in the driveway.

Months passed and I noticed that this lady had left all of her important, personal documentation in drawers as if she left suddenly. I mean, who divorces someone based upon what he told me and leaves everything behind: dishes, furniture, documentation on their children, etc.? It didn't seem logical but he got angry and agitated whenever I questioned him so I would just leave it alone.

Everywhere we went, even at church, I was treated like "the other woman." People looked down at me but I didn't understand why. Word started circulating that he had been cheating on his ex-wife with a young lady he worked with who also attended the same church. That was when all hell broke loose for me. He started drinking and accusing me of flirting with people at work nearly every day. The ladies in my office were envious of me and I was a nervous wreck. I hoped that no male from work recognized me during my lunch hour because if they said hello I would get called names and cursed out on the drive back to work and even worse when I got home.

I remember being so impressed with how many African Americans drove really nice cars in Atlanta. I would look out the window as we drove to church just admiring different cars and suddenly got accused and cursed out for checking out some random man. "What Man?" I would utter. I was in shock. I tried to tell a lady who I had befriended at work about what I was going through. She was older than me and had the same name as my mom. I was hoping she would be like a mom to me but when she saw him and how I acted when I was with him she became afraid and basically stopped speaking or hanging with me. I was so alone.

I got a new job at a different company, paying more. I thought he would be as excited as I was. I would get dressed and ask, "How do I look?" Whatever I put on for work was not good enough. He had to style my hair every morning in an old lady style. He stalked me by coming to my job every day for lunch and if a man from work saw us and spoke to me he would start accusing me again, this time right on the spot. Friday nights were horrible. I got cursed out and called funky this and that or a whoremonger. As my pay increased, so did the abuse. He would say, "Why does God keep blessing you more than he does me?" Within that same week, we had a guest speaker come to church and he called me out and made me turn and face the back of the church. "Oh Lord, he's back there in the sound room I thought to myself." The evangelist said, "The Lord told me to tell you that the reason he blesses you more than he does others is because you are obedient and faithful to him." People began to clap and my husband got so angry. Inside I thought, "Wow God, you want me to know that you see me."

When I got a new job at Coca Cola, immediately he accused me of "skinning and grinning" at my coworkers. I loved that place and my manager. She was great! The first week of work was awesome until one day I had to work late and I could not remember what street I came into to get in the parking garage. The parking garage was so huge I got lost. I was terrified as I walked from one deck to the next. An old Caucasian gentleman who looked like an executive pulled up beside me and urged me to get in the car so that he could help me. He assured me that it was much more dangerous to be walking that garage than to be with him. As I got in the car the scripture that came to my mind was Hebrews 13:2, "Be not forgetful to entertain strangers: for thereby some have entertained angels unawares." He drove me around the parking deck until I saw my car. Well, by then it was dark outside and I was even more terrified of what was waiting for me when I got home. I was greeted with a screeching, "Where have you been!" When I explained what happened, I got called a liar along with all kinds of names. I told him that none of this was making any sense and I asked him why was he so angry. Overwhelmed and confused, I grabbed my jacket and attempted to leave to take a ride to the grocery store. I had nowhere else to go because I didn't know anybody and was not allowed to get to know anybody. This guy who promised to love, honor and cherish me, picked me up by my jacket and threw me into a brick wall yelling, "You are not going anywhere! I told your a*s not to be playin' with me!" I sat there in shock trying to catch my breath. Then I went to the bedroom and did what I knew to do. I dropped on my knees and prayed.

WHAM! Out of nowhere came a slap across my head that made me see stars. I thought that type of thing only happened in the cartoons. "Oh my LORD!" I shouted. "Get up off of your knees!" he yelled. I shuffled hysterically into the corner as he stood over me screaming profane words. I cried and wished it was a bad dream but it wasn't. How could this be happening? We go to church every Sunday! We hear the songs and sermons! What is wrong and why doesn't any one of these Holy Ghost-filled people see in the

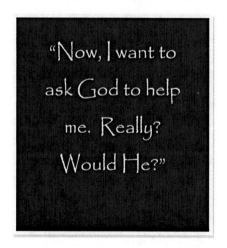

spirit what is happening to me? In shock, I was still trying to process what happened. I was numb and like a zombie the next day. My head was still swimming from the blow. This can't be happening to me! I thought to myself. Not Me! I felt so alone, ashamed to even ask God to help me because I didn't ask Him about marrying this man. Now I want to ask God to help me. Really? Would He? What I didn't realize at the time was that God's word says in Jeremiah 33:3 "Call unto me, and I will answer thee, and shew thee great and mighty things, which thou knowest not." Psalms 20:1 "The Lord hear thee in the day of trouble; the name of the God of Jacob defend thee" and my personal favorite that gave me hope in what seemed to be a hopeless situation was Psalms 50:15 "...call upon me in the day of trouble: I will deliver thee, and thou shalt glorify me."

The women on my job would tell me how sweet it was for my husband to come share my lunch hour with me and how much they wished that their husbands would come meet them for lunch each day. What they didn't know was he was an abuser and accused me daily of liking someone on the job and because of it I could not have lunch like any normal person. There was no choice as to who I was having lunch with because he was there spying on me.

One day we were at McDonalds for lunch and one of the guys from the office walked up to the counter beside me and said hello. I was frozen inside. My stomach got so sick because all I heard was, "Um Hum." I knew that meant a beaten when I got home. That went on for at least five years. It didn't matter what job I had, on Friday's it would be worse. I could not understand it because he was supposed to be such a Christian, such a prayer warrior. But when I listened to his prayers, they didn't even make sense. They were some kind of rhymes and mixed up, crazy words that were spoken really fast. I said, "Lord, how did I miss this?" Someone can make you think they are so holy when they are actually religious and ritualistic with no relationship with the Messiah Jesus. However when you don't take time to ask questions or listen to Holy Spirit you overlook the signs and alarms in your heart that say, "This is not right! Don't do it!" Denial and self-doubt will come in when you hear yourself saying, "I must be mistaken. That didn't really happen. He didn't mean it. What did I do to trigger this?"

I was no longer the person I once knew myself to be. In fact, this was the beginning of how my weekends would be for the next two years. That young, ambitious, vibrant lady that I used to be swam deep down within and just shut down. Still in shock, I could not speak for weeks and I went to church and worshipped with my eyes closed. I hated the person that I had become. In fact, I didn't even recognize myself anymore when I looked in the mirror. I was always looking in the mirror. Maybe it was because I was looking for the real me but it was also easy to see when he was going to walk up on me and I could quickly read his facial expressions. I began to hide knives in the window seals. My life was similar to that movie, *Sleeping with the Enemy*. The lady in that movie could not have a can out of place in the cupboard. She couldn't do this or that in her own home. It was so real to me because I was living that way. He had old furniture that seemed like it was from the 1970s era with oil lamps and a custom plastic covering on the burnt orange sofa with white trim and weird looking tables. I remember thinking to myself, "Why is this junk so special?" I remember walking with my toes up in the air because the carpet was so icky. My feet began to change and they started to peel. Even the mattress was nasty. It was built up by quilts. It made me feel sick when I changed the linens. On top of all of that, I began to get infections, sometimes yeast and sometimes vaginal bacterial. One year, I was on antibiotics so much for infections that my gynecologist told me that I needed to have my husband checked. He didn't care how swollen I was or how much pain I was in, he still insisted on having sex. I felt like a slut or a rape victim. Finally he went to the doctor after a year and a half of me pleading with him about it. Sure enough, he was diagnosed with a fungus on his penis that needed to come off. For years, he had me believing that it was a scar that had developed from when he and a woman from his past had sex so long that it ripped and healed that way. He got the surgery and once he was healed, it was on then! He was like a drug addict, but sex was addiction. I could not understand it at the time.

"I didn't want anyone to go to jail because of me, so I kept silent."

I wasn't allowed to go anywhere alone except to the grocery store. I couldn't even go to the mall by myself. It was so bad that I could barely go to church by myself. Meanwhile, I became active in the church. I didn't talk to many people because of the scandalous story about him and the coworker who was a member of the church. It was hard to know who I could trust. Soon, I became a Sunday School teacher for teens. It helped me escape my pain. I studied the Bible and prayed a lot for Sunday School class. I felt so alone. I could not tell my family what happened to me because of what happened to Auntie Fuzzy. I thought they would be angry with me and they would kill him. I didn't want anyone to go to jail because of me, so I kept silent.

The cycle of abuse continued and escalated to the point that he pressed a knife into my throat, bragging that he could easily kill me and nobody would know because of the amount of space between houses. He warned me that he had been in prison before and did not care about going back. Visions of Auntie Fuzzy came to me but I still never told anyone what was happening to me for over five years. I wish I could say that I learned something from that summer day or from Auntie Fuzzy's experience and because of that I avoided a domestic violent situation, but the truth of the matter is, I didn't. Thank God for sending my brother to Atlanta to help me see my life through another set of lenses.

CHAPTER 3
IT WASN'T THE FIRST TIME

Now that I think about it, that wasn't my first time. Remember when I stated that it didn't matter if it was your first time or second time witnessing domestic violence that it doesn't guarantee that you will not become a victim yourself? Well, I dated a police officer who got out of control when he started drinking. One night he came to my door and I heard Holy Spirit clearly say, "Do not let him in." I replied, "I got this God." Holy Spirit will always warn us but sometimes we ignore his voice. Some of you have been there too, haven't you? I opened the door even after seeing him staggering. As soon as he stepped in, he pulled out his pistol and pushed me in front of the mirror that was in my foyer and said to me, "How does it feel to have cold iron on your skin?" I was nervous as I thought to myself if this gun goes off nobody will know what happened to me. Guess what I did next? You know it! I started praying to God asking him to forgive me for not listening and to get me out of this situation. I was afraid to move suddenly for fear of the gun accidentally going off. I looked him in the eyes through the mirror and said, "You need to get out of here right now in the Name of Jesus!" He chuckled and said he wasn't going to hurt me for real. When he stepped out that door I never let him in my life again. That night my life flashed before me and I thought of my auntie. He would call and try to speak to me out in public. Although he was very apologetic I NEVER dealt with him again.

Whenever you are simply dating someone like I described, there is a possibility that you can walk away. But after you've said 'I do', in my mind it was more difficult because my mom used to always say, "It's easy and doesn't cost much to say 'I do' but it costs you a whole lot more to get in a marriage and realize you've made a mistake." I've escaped an abusive relationship once and here I am in a marriage worse than the previous relationship. I didn't ask the Lord about this marriage. It was purely a decision of the flesh and because of that I felt trapped. My prayer life developed over time because I only had God to talk to about what was going on in my life.

I thank God for the author of the mini-book that I found in the bookstore. I recall titles such as: "Breaking Controlling Powers!" Oh my God! I began to pray the prayers in that book. Visiting the bookstore at church became my safe haven. That one visit changed my life forever. Eventually, I became a bookstore volunteer and would read every new book that came in. I found another book entitled, "Overcoming the Spirit of Insecurity." After reading that book, I realized that my husband had a spirit of insecurity and I began to come against and loose that demon by the power of Holy Spirit. Finally, I got the courage to tell him that I was joining the church choir. Of course the accusations began again. "Well, you just want to join the choir because you like the musician!" I spoke directly to the spirit, "Devil, I'm going to join the choir and I come against that spirit of insecurity! You will not hold me hostage any longer, in the Name of Jesus!" That week I joined the choir. It was the BEST thing for me. Worship was a way of escape from my hostage relationship. The songs that the choir sang back then just meant so much to me, like "There is no way I can live without you" and "Joy, Joy, God's great joy, down in my soul." That's where I needed God to reach and rescue me, down in my soul! A song used to come to mind after a horrible weekend of name calling and hitting. It was titled, "I Must Tell Jesus." The lyrics went something like, *"I must tell Jesus all of my troubles. I cannot bear these burdens alone. In my distress He always will help me. Jesus will help me. Jesus alone!"* The loneliness began to subside as I just worshipped Jesus. I thought I was hiding the truth of what was happening to me as a form of protecting my family because I didn't want them to get hurt or to kill him. But that was really a trick and a lie from Satan to keep me isolated. Yet, the more the abuse occurred, the more I studied the bible, the more I fasted, the more I prayed until the power of Holy Spirit totally consumed me. Over this period of time, I realized that I didn't have a relationship with Jesus like I thought. My relationship with the Lord grew stronger to the point that I was able to overcome that controlling power operating in this abusive man I had married. It seemed as though the more I grew spiritually, his threats and abuse intensified. How does this happen in the lives of people who are very active in the church? I mean, he was like the right hand man to the Bishop. He would ensure that he looked good before he went out of his office by clipping his hair and shaping his beard. I was like the Bishop's daughter. We talked all the time and I trusted him like a father. Yet we had such dysfunction going on at home that nobody at church recognized it or at least acknowledged it. He even started having affairs with women in the church. These women would call me at work and harass me, come up to me after church and say nasty things to me. Other women who I looked up to would gossip about me as if I was the other woman and saying that I should not be allowed to teach Sunday School. I could not understand why the people at church would not embrace me as a new member in the community.

Just when I thought it couldn't get any worse, it did. One morning after he drove off, I whispered to God, "Lord, let him get killed in an accident so that I can be free." Suddenly a Sheriff pulled up in the driveway and I started repenting. I knew I shouldn't have said that. The Sheriff was actually delivering divorce papers to him. On top of being an abuser, this man was a bigamist. He had forged his divorce papers. It was unreal. That's why she left all of her important papers and didn't take anything that should have been important to divorced woman. I was about to go on a two-year journey that would explain it all.

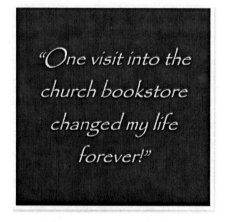

"One visit into the church bookstore changed my life forever!"

When he came home and I presented the documents to him, he had a weird smirk on his face and said she was lying and that the cult church she was a member of was putting her up to it. I believed him. One winter day, he suggested that we get rid of old papers and burn them as heat in the wood burning stove that we had. I did not realize that it was getting closer to the trial date. I was reading things as we burned them and I would ask him questions about why she didn't take the documents and why we were burning them. He got so agitated that I would back off but for some reason I knew that I was going to need a copy of her signature for something so I was going to save one of the cancelled checks.

Thank God for Holy Spirit! Sure enough, after going through three attorneys and several delays, I called the last one and asked why they dropped him and they said that they simply could not represent him given the evidence. We received another attorney who just ignored us for months. I called him and asked him why. He told me that the case was going to be hard to fight. I asked why so he scheduled a meeting with us and asked him in front of me about the forgery. He and a business partner had forged his divorce papers. I was flabbergasted because that was one of the documents that I asked to see before I was willing to marry him. I read it. I saw his signature and what I thought was his ex-wife's signature. When I went home that day, I pulled out that old check with her signature on it and realized that it was NOT her signature. OMG! I was even angrier that he had the nerve to accuse me of all kinds of stuff. What have I gotten myself into? "GOD, help me!" I cried.

I think his feeling guilty led him to take it out on me even more with verbal and physical abuse. In the midst of all of this, I found out that my father was diagnosed with cancer. And then an evangelist that I was very close with diagnosed with cancer as well and died. Her family asked me to read a scripture as part of the funeral service. Right before I went up to read the scripture, my husband whispered in my ear, "I want a divorce." Can you imagine the emotions that ran through my head? I don't think you can. Some of you may be thinking, good riddance! In fact, I was hurt, body shaking, and trying to fight back the tears from grief both from my dear friend's death, the reminder of my father's mortality, listening to her family crying, and hearing his voice ringing divorce in my ears. Emotionally drained, I said to the Lord, "Father, you are going to have to help me. I can't keep doing this!" I wanted to fall on the floor and just give up on life myself but Holy Spirit was there holding me up.

Within the same year, my father passed away and left me an inheritance. Still trying to make the marriage work with this man, I spent a few thousand dollars remodeling and upgrading the home with new carpet, new kitchen counters, new blinds, and new furniture but he still would not allow me to go in the living room. After we got all of the upgrades completed, he told me that I had to move out or he was going to kill me. "What did you say?" I asked. "You heard me. I am going to kill you if you don't get out!" he replied. I asked about all of this money that I just spent to upgrade this house and buy new furniture? He said, "Somebody will use it but it will not be you."

Months later, my husband divorce case with his ex was set to go before a judge. I was so nervous because the only thing I remember about this lady is that crazy grocery store experience where the guy was screaming that I was going to hell. We had to go into a room where she was. I remember praying and hearing in my spirit, "You have an advocate going with you and the winds will shift in your direction." When we entered the room, my husband started speaking to his ex-wife harshly like he did me. She responded to him just like me. In fact, I said to myself, "She's just like me." I realized that she was not the enemy. He got up and walked out of the room leaving me in there with his not so ex-wife. She began to speak to me about the goodness of the Lord. I had mixed emotions of confusion and relief. The attorneys came to an agreement that she had a right to come to the house and take everything that was hers. Guess what? That boiled down to everything that wasn't mine. Including that old 1970s furniture in the living room. "Yay!" I thought.

By the time all this was to be carried out, my brother had moved down from Kentucky. He was living with us. He was recovering from a hard time back home. The court ordered my husband not to be present when the ex-wife came to the house to recover her things. She told me that the reason why she left was because he had threatened to kill her and she believed him since he had tried it before. I knew she wasn't lying because he had pulled a knife on me before and told me that he would stab me. Through my tears, all I knew to do was whisper within and remind God of His holy word! I said, "Lord, your word says no weapon formed against me shall prosper so if he stabbed me I need to see how you will not allow this to prosper."

Suddenly, he put the knife down and said, "I'm not going to stab you," and walked away. Plus she didn't know that he had just threatened to kill me. She asked me if she could take me for a drive to show me something the Lord wanted me to see. While driving, she told me how he abused her and cheated on her with a young lady at his church. This was the same young lady whose mother was harassing me. She continued to say that he would seem like he was changed and truly giving his all to the Lord then slowly he would begin to start getting agitated, and acting indifferent towards her. He stopped going to church, then the threats of death would begin. That's when she knew he was cheating. I was experiencing the same thing. I wished I could tell her but I was too ashamed. She continued to drive and talk. She said that she gathered what she could and got her son and left when he wasn't home. She didn't care what she had to leave behind, she just escaped with her life. Nevertheless, she said the Lord restored all that she had lost because she put the money down on the house, purchased all of the furniture and appliances then he wanted her to leave. Well, that also sounded familiar. It was a pattern. She said that the Lord restored everything that was taken from her and she showed me the house she moved into. It was very nice. She told me about how the Lord allowed her to purchase a beautiful horse ranch and she refurnished her homes. Then she said something that gave me hope. She said, "The Lord told me to tell you that He is going to do the same for you." As we went back to the house, I was encouraged that the Lord sent this lady to tell me that He saw me and was going to deliver me.

We arrived back to the house. Both my brother and I had to help this lady that I did not know, who had just been divorced from the man that I was married to for four years move her stuff, stuff that I couldn't even sit on. Really Jesus? Thank God for my brother's patience. I was thankful for God's grace!

The ex-wife told me that she intended to take all of the appliances but because she knew that I was innocent in this situation she was leaving the washer, dryer, oven and refrigerator for my sake. After it was all over, I hid by taking a shower, crying and washing over and over again. I wanted to just die. When he came home, all he could say was, "Do you have plans to move out and have you decided what you

"She didn't care what she had to leave behind, she just escaped with her life!"

are taking?" I was so disgusted! I said to him, "Look around you, whatever you are unable to put in a trash bag is what I'm taking." He was so angry and started cursing and calling me names. I prayed and let the devil know that he no longer had control over me.

There were so many red flags that I overlooked because I yielded to carnality, not recognizing the seeds that I was planting towards my future. Galatians 6:8 AMP says, *"For the one who sows to his flesh [his sinful capacity, his worldliness, his disgraceful impulses] will reap from the flesh ruin and destruction, but the one who sows to the Spirit will from the Spirit reap eternal life."* Through much prayer and after nearly two more years of that kind of life, I was freed from a life of domestic violence. But how? The process to breaking free, staying free, and being free is what we will explore further.

CHAPTER 4
LET'S BREAK THE CYCLE

You CAN be FREE! Really and unquestionably free! There is a way of escape and hope for you. Hallelujah!

The day that Proverbs 18:21 *"Death and life are in the power of the tongue, And those who love it and indulge it will eat its fruit and bear the consequences of their words"* became my powerful truth. I started to speak life in and around my situation with the fruit and consequences following. My first prayer was "Lord if he raises his hands to hit me again, cause his arm to be cut off!" Quickly I repented and said, *"No Lord don't do that because then he will not be able to work."* Then I said, *"Lord, show me that you hear me. If he even thinks of hitting me, cause his arm to receive a pain in it so badly that he would wish that it were cut off."* One evening he got angry and started balling up his fist and was about to hit me. I could feel the intensity building. Suddenly, he grabbed his arm and started complaining about it hurting. The pain got so intense that he had to go to the doctor and he literally said that he wished it was cut off! I told him that it was the hand of the Lord. I said, *"God told me that you will never hit me again and if you do He will deal with you in this way."* He never hit me again.

The physical abuse ended but the verbal abuse continued. It seemed as though the emotional abuse would last longer than the physical abuse because those scars were not visible. It didn't matter where we were, he would say hurtful things to me.

One night during a revival at our church the evangelist called me out and says, "God is going to do something for you. You are about to give birth!" I was so SHOCKED! I wanted to scream NO LORD! *I asked you to rescue me!* For so many years, this man has been wanting me to have a baby and my prayer was always, Lord if you love me, please don't allow me to have a child by this man. What does this prophecy mean? Right behind that service there was another minister who I valued and loved called me out in front of the congregation and said, "God is going to turn your mess into a message and He's anointing you to tell women what you are going through. It will be a Women's Ministry." It later became clear to me that the ability to help women like me, and

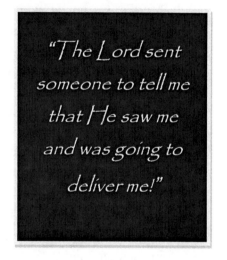

"The Lord sent someone to tell me that He saw me and was going to deliver me!"

like you break free and stay free from domestic violence was the birthing that the evangelist saw.

Beloved, whatever mess that you are in right now can and will become a message for someone even in the form of a testimony. You CAN break free TODAY beloved! The scripture that comes to mind is Acts 3:19AMP *"So repent [change your inner self—your old way of thinking, regret past sins] and return [to God—seek His purpose for your life], so that your sins may be wiped away [blotted out, completely erased], so that times of refreshing may come from the presence of the Lord [restoring you like a cool wind on a hot day]"*

Breaking free starts with your inner self, your mind.

1. Simply repent to change one's mind for better, heartily to amend with abhorrence of one's past sins). When you take this step the accusations Satan has been using against you all of this time will be brought to an end. It could be a prayer like this one, "Heavenly Father, I come to you now acknowledging that I need you. Forgive me Father for placing myself in the position to be in this type of relationship and for placing anyone before you as my Lord and Savior. Lord Jesus please come into my heart. I welcome you to sit on the throne of my heart forever. Holy Spirit lead and guide me from this day forward into all truth. I accept your instruction and will follow you. Thank you Heavenly Father for accepting me into your Kingdom and into the body/family of Christ my Lord, In the Name of Jesus Christ, Amen." You no longer have to feel alone or afraid.

2. Start Over with God. Amend your relationship with GOD. Oh YES! There is such a thing as a Do-Over honey! Hallelujah! All roads travelled on your search for significance and purpose in life leads to Him through faith in Jesus Christ not a man or a woman. Experience times of refreshing by reading and meditating on scriptures in the Holy Bible. Visit a local Christian or church bookstore and select the

best study bible for you and purchase a prayer journal. We establish relationships with someone by spending time with them. Spend time having conversations with your Heavenly Father, spend time being quiet to hear how the scriptures speak to you and His Holy Spirit speaks to you, then write it in your journal for later reflection and encouragement. You have been in a very hot situation but it is time for a refreshing to pour into your life like a cool wind. Guess what? You may not have even moved out of the house yet but you have changed addresses; mentally and spiritually!

3. Believe. Believe that your sins and your past mistakes are completely erased. Believe that God forgives you when you repent. Your family has been painstakingly waiting for you to come out of this so don't even think they will not forgive you. More importantly YOU must Believe in YOU again and forgive YOURSELF! Go ahead. Say it now. "I forgive myself for allowing myself to ignore the signs, accept abusive treatment, expose my children to this pain, and stay longer than I should have. I'm Breaking Free, Staying Free, and Living FREE from this day forward! I believe in ME." It's not too late for you! Hey, I was only 25 years old when I got into this marriage to this man who was nearly double my age. I felt like I had lost the best years of my life at that time. I was not allowed to go to college. I could only go to work and church. However, the Lord placed me in the church

bookstore which was filled with every book on every subject so it was like going to a bible college. But GOD! I started fasting, praying, worshipping, and setting the atmosphere for the presence of God to be welcomed in my home. God's presence was so heavy it would fill the house to the point that it would feel like I had the heat on in the room. Every spirit had to be subject to the presence of the Lord of Hosts and I was refreshed. Thank God for TBN at the time because I would have TBN on or a good preaching tape playing before he came in. He would say, "Um Hum. God is protecting you today but I'm going to get you tomorrow." I would just laugh on the inside at Satan. Only God can give you that kind of strength and peace.

4. Don't go back. Look for and take the way of escape that God will provide. Let the Lord lead you to the person that you can speak with about what's going on. Tell someone that you can trust, that has authority and the ability to help you without judging or manipulating you based on what is happening to you. Don't continue to allow Satan's spirit of shame to hold you in a secret hostage state. Trust me! You are not the first person who has gone through this that God has rescued! I'm alive to tell you that HE WILL make a way of escape for you! Hallelujah, Glory to God! Thank you Jesus! 1 Corinthians 10:13 AMP "No temptation [regardless of its source] has overtaken or enticed you that is not common to human experience [nor is any

temptation unusual or beyond human resistance]; but God is faithful [to His word—He is compassionate and trustworthy], and He will not let you be tempted beyond your ability [to resist], but along with the temptation He [has in the past and is now and] will [always] provide the way out as well, so that you will be able to endure it [without yielding, and will overcome temptation with joy]." When God makes the way of escape, the way out for you, honey you and your children run for your life and don't look back. Don't even go back to get some item you think is important! I did this even after my pastor warned me not to. I told myself I am going back one last time to get whatever it was that was important to me and I left raped. Don't even go back to get items you think are important! I did this even after my pastor warned me not to. I told myself I am going back one last time to get whatever it was that was important to me and I left raped. I can't believe that even after all of that I still went back. I even renewed my vows with this man. One day out of nowhere my husband at that time came to me and said, "The Lord told me to leave you for 7 days." I went to a wise woman at our church who knew what was going on. I asked her what I should do. She said, "Honey, take the keys to your car and your house from him. Let him Go and don't look back." What do you think I did? Well, I followed her instructions BUT after a day or so, he called and wanted to have breakfast at the house. Once he got in there I could hardly get him out. I had to call the police, when they came they initially thought I was the one causing the disturbance because I was so shaken and upset. It took some time to convince them that I was not the offender. When they realized that he had threatened to kill me and had previously abused me their perspective changed. Why do you think women are initially seen as the aggressor when the authorities arrive? Other sisters shared that they also called the police, but they were actually arrested instead of the abuser because the police saw

> "When God makes the way of escape, the way out for you, honey you and your children run for your life and don't look back!"

scratches on the abuser, due to them trying to defend themselves. They were charged with all kinds of things and could not get bailed out because there was a restraining order on the abusers and they had alienated themselves from their family and friends.   What are some do's and don'ts in this situation?

- DO make a formal report when you have been abused. I believe I went to the magistrate court and filed a complaint that he was abusing me and threatened to kill me so that if I had to defend myself they would know what was going on. This was suggested by an attorney.

- DO make others aware as I've said before. Let your Human Resources department and your pastor know in the event the person comes on your job or does something at church.   They have to keep it confidential.

- DO let the 911 operator know it is a domestic violence situation that is escalating and that YOU are fearful for your life so that it is recorded that you are in danger.

- DO try to calm down when the officers arrive so that you can calmly express yourself. Once I calmed down and explained that he was an adulterer, bigamist, and that it was documented that he had threatened to kill me they changed their tone with me and began to deal with him. I told them that he was yelling before they arrived, even if he wasn't doing it then. Once I disengaged with him he could not hold it any longer and he began yelling and acting crazy in front of the police.

- DON'T believe the lie that this is what love is and

that you may have deserved it or did something to trigger this level of response.

- DON'T believe the lie that this was a one-time thing and it will never happen again.

- DON'T believe the lie that you need to leave first and come back for the children. NO! The LORD will provide for ALL of you to escape together! Remember, your first and second step. Put away all old patterns of thinking and behaviors of manipulation. God is going to use his angelic hosts to break you out!

Take note that even when you have been liberated in your mind and spirit the abuser may come at you and try to hurt you again but there's POWER in the Name of Jesus. One time the abusive man I had married came in angry and picked me up over his head and was about to slam me down and I shouted, "Jesus, Save Me!" Slowly, he put me down placing me back on my feet and walked away. Even after I had gotten this new liberation and was waiting for the open door to leave there were still times when it seemed like Satan had the upper hand. Let me put a pin right there. Don't use the "waiting for an escape" as an excuse. When the Father provides the escape, take it! Too many people make excuses to stay!

Still wavering in my decision even after I had left my ex-husband, I was reminded of a dream that I had right before I made the final decision to leave. It was one of those dreams that I have where I see what is to come. I've had them all of my life even when I was not living for the

Lord as I should. In this dream, my ex-husband and I were sleeping when suddenly I heard someone come into our home through the front door. I could hear their footsteps dragging the floor with an eerie sound of death. It sounded like a person walking in very heavy boots like my brother used to wear when he worked in a deep freezer. I could hear each step the person took as they were coming closer to our bedroom. I remember in the dream frantically searching for a place to hide. I said to my ex-husband, *we need to hide they are coming to kill us. I can fill it.* There was no place for me to hide. As the person got to the doorway, I could see the silhouette of a man's body. He came towards me and began to try to kill me. I remember in the dream shouting my ex-husband's name and yelling, *"Call 911! Call 911!"* He assumed a stance like a zombie and dropped his hands to his sides. As the man and I struggled somehow I received supernatural strength and wrestled this strong man down to the floor, face down, arms behind his back with my knees in the palms of his hands. When the lights came on and I looked at the man it was my ex-husband! In shock I said, *"It's YOU! There are two of you and you are trying to kill me!"* In the dream my ex-husband just stood there with no life in him. I heard the voice of the Lord say, "Bind the strong man." I had no idea what this dream meant. All I knew was that I had to get out of there.

After I moved out, my ex-husband kept asking to see me. I told him that I would only see him at a church service. We agreed to meet at a small church in Atlanta where Juanita Bynum was conducting a revival. She was preaching and her subject was "Binding the Strongman."

Her text was from Mark 3:23-27KJV: "And he called them unto him, and said unto them in parables, How can Satan cast out Satan? And if a kingdom be divided against itself, that kingdom cannot stand. And if a house be divided against itself, that house cannot stand. And if Satan rise up against himself, and be divided, he cannot stand, but hath an end. No man can enter into a strong man's house, and spoil his goods, except he will first bind the strong man; and then he will spoil his house." That dream and those words came back to me! It became clear what that statement meant as she taught. I realized that the strong man was the stronghold that had my ex-husband in bondage and it was trying to destroy us both.

After the service, I was able to thank the woman of God for that message. With her was a short lady dressed in African attire who interceded for her the entire service as she preached. I had met her once before at a church service where she was interceding for this same person. The lady remembered my name. She spoke very deliberately, "Sister Tina, I remember you. In fact, I have been praying for you and the Lord showed me that you were in a very violent storm. There was turmoil all around you but I saw the Lord pick you up and place you into the eye of the storm and nothing could hurt you. When storms are raging, planes actually fly into the eye of the storm and its calm there. Did you know that? I answered no. She went on to say that the storm that she saw me in had to do with a man. Then she turned and asked, "Who is this with you?" Uncomfortable and embarrassed I introduced him as my estranged husband. They both said, "Uh Huh" at the same time. She took my number and told me she would call me to pray. That night I left with certainty that the decision I had made to move on with my life was saving my life. I realized that even though it seemed like I was in the ICU the Lord was saying to me, "I See You and I am bringing you to a place of peace and healing." As the song "In His Safety" by Lecresia Campbell comes to my mind, I pray that this story that I've shared is used to encourage you today to break free, stay free and BE free. The storms of life may be raging in your life but as Psalm 91 encourages you, the song and my story reminds you that you can move forward with wisdom resting in the safety of the Lord Jehovah Nissi, God our Banner and Protection!

CHAPTER 5
EXCUSES WOMEN AND MEN USE TO STAY

Why do you think women or men stay longer than they should in abusive relationships? I've often heard it said sometimes even after the person has been murdered, "What in the world was she/he thinking? Why didn't they leave?" One of the main reasons is finances. People think they can't afford to leave. Can you afford to stay? I happened to get an attorney who said to me, "I don't know why but I'm not going to charge you because this is dangerous for you. He said, this man is so coy that he's telling you to your face what he's doing to you and blatantly doing it in the open. You don't have anything tying you to this man, not even a dog. I'm going to help you break free of him and keep what you have because you have lost enough! However, if you go back to this man you will have to pay me every red cent." I remember calling the attorney telling him, "*He said he's going to kill himself if I don't see him again!*" The attorney was so calm and said, "Dear, he loves himself too much and the life he's been living off of you. He's not going to kill himself. He will kill you! Stay away from him, in fact, I want you to come to my office." I went to the attorney's office and he reminded me of our conversation over the phone then he instructed me to call the police whenever he comes near me. Never open the door if he comes to your home without having a witness or someone there with you. I responded to the attorney, "*But I have a restraining order.*" He pulled out a large pistol from his desk drawer and slammed it down beside a sheet of paper. He said, "Do you know how many women have been killed over a sheet of paper? A bullet does not recognize a piece of paper. Some people see a restraining order as a piece of paper. You've got to restrain yourself! You've got to manage the relationship and set the proper boundaries." That was a wakeup call for me and I know it is for you right now. You have not been setting proper boundaries in relationships and the time to start is now! You have to set proper boundaries even when it comes to seeking out help. I left the attorney's office and called a close friend and had them come meet me to talk things over. Be careful not to turn to that person of the opposite sex for comfort and consolation during such a vulnerable time even if it is a church member. You can easily find yourself getting involved with them unintentionally. Not that I did that but I was warned that it could happen and has happened to others. I thank God for saints in my life that warned me and held me accountable in this area.

Once you've gotten away from the abuser and if that person attempts to come back to your home or place of employment or even if you are driving down the road and they start following you call the police. Keep on calling them until the person gets the message. My skin would feel like it was on fire when I heard the doorbell ring and it was him outside my door yelling for me to let him in. I would stand in the hallway in terror but I would manage to call 911 and they would ask him to leave. I've had to pull off into a beauty supply before and ask them to call the police because I was being followed by a person who had threatened to kill me. I went behind the counter with the clerk and they picked up the phone to call the police. Don't worry about the police getting angry. Tell them that you do not feel safe, the person has a history of domestic violence towards you and you need their help and protection. I'm telling you I did it until I stopped feeling like a prisoner in my own house, in my own skin. I did it until I could say go away and mean it! Eventually he stopped coming because he knew I meant it.

You may be thinking about what or how your escape will look to the church. "What are they going to think about me? What if they think it was my fault? Everybody loved him so they will not believe me?" These were all once my concerns too. In fact, during our 7th year of marriage my brother came to live with us and he worked in the salon we owned. One day my precious brother came home from work and gave me a flower that he could barely afford. He told me that I needed to open my eyes and look into what was going on. I told him that I was not going to try to track that down because Jesus made me a promise in his Word about secrets.

Mark 4:22 AMP *For **nothing is hidden**, except to be revealed; nor has anything been **kept secret**, but that it would come to light [that is, things are hidden only temporarily, until the appropriate time comes for them to be known].*

Luke 8:17 AMP *For there is **nothing hidden** that will not become evident, **nor anything secret** that will not be known and come out into the open.*

Luke 12:2 AMP *But there is **nothing [so carefully] concealed** that it will not be revealed, nor **so hidden** that it will not be made known.*

The writer of the book of Hebrews concurs with Christ by saying, *Nothing in all the world can be hidden from God. Everything is clear and lies open before him. And to him we must explain the way we have lived.* Hebrews 4:13 International Children's Bible. Honey, this means when God snatches the covers off of people you cannot pull those things up from the toes baby! Sure enough God began to expose things in our marriage and about the man I had married. Sure there were some people who came up to me and accused me of not being a good wife, but I simply let them know in a nice way that they were not walking in L.O.V.E. "Living On Valid Evidence." Let's make sure that it is not you or I in church judging people based upon false evidence. If our life is based upon Christ's love then we will see and BE L.O.V.E. to others. That love covers a multitude of sin and casts out all F.E.A.R., False Evidence Appearing Real.

Listen, I'm not telling you that exposure doesn't hurt. It was painful for me. I was well known, liked, and active in ministry. I remember telling God, *"Lord, you are killing me! Why are you exposing ME in front of all of these people?"* His

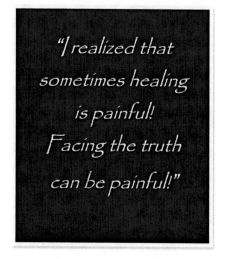

"I realized that sometimes healing is painful! Facing the truth can be painful!"

response was, "You said you wanted to be like Jesus." I told him that I could not be like Jesus and I didn't even want to be like Jesus. I just wanted this to end. Just kill me if you are not going to get me out of this! You will need that same L.O.V.E. I mentioned to stand in faith and forgive your abuser. S it is when healing a broken bone or a deep cut, I realized that healing emotionally is painful.

CHAPTER 6
REAL LIFE STORIES

I felt it was necessary to broaden the scope by bringing in other women to share their experiences with overcoming domestic violence and the excuses they used. These are real life stories as told by women who were empowered by God's truth to break free and are now staying free!

Vickie's Story:

Q: Why do women ignore the initial signs of abuse?

A: I honestly thought it was an isolated incident and I provoked it to happen so I let the first fight slide. He was crying and very apologetic and I thought he was sincere and it wouldn't happen again. It didn't happen for a few months until I moved in with him, then I found myself "stuck."

Q: What excuses do women use to stay in a relationship?

A: I didn't make excuses. I hid the abuse by staying out of the public eye and staying away from friends when I was beaten so I wouldn't have to make an excuse.

Q: What excuse did YOU use to stay?

A: I convinced myself that this was love and no one else would ever want me so I might as well stay. When I convinced myself that this wasn't love and I was ready to get out of the situation, I'd get a job to have some income and two paychecks to get an apartment. Unfortunately, every time I got a job my ex would beat me up so bad that I would miss days of work due to black eyes and usually I'd get fired within the first three months. This would happen over and over again.

Q: What was your breaking point?
A: I never called the police on my ex, even after I almost died and had to be hospitalized through the fourth of July. I never told anyone. One day, he threatened me and I knew he was going to hit me so I told him I was going to call the cops. He assumed I was bluffing so he kept on. Finally, I had enough and I called the cops. The cops questioned both of us and decided to lock me up due to a scratch on his arm that was caused by me after trying to restrain him from hitting me. They locked me up with a laundry list of misdemeanors including something like child cruelty (or some sort of charge like that) since his child witnessed us fighting. He wasn't allowed to come bail me out of jail since a restraining order against me was filed due to the charges that were imposed by the state, not my "ex" who was the abuser. I had no family or friends to come bail me out. I pushed all my friends away and didn't want my parents to find out. A total stranger (which happened to be a bail bondsman) got me out of jail and mentioned a battered women's shelter that could help. Although I didn't have a job and no support system, I made the decision to leave him at that point even if I had to be homeless. And that is exactly what I did after 8 years of physical, mental, and sexual abuse.

Q: What scriptures, if any did you rely on during and after the relationship?

A: Although I had back-slid and didn't have a close relationship with God, I often reminded myself to read 1 Corinthians 13:4-8. I read it often, to try to convince myself that this was NOT love and would read it to my "Ex" as well. I also prayed the prayer of Jabez often in 1 Chronicles 4:10, usually at night before bed.

Q: Did you seek help? If so who and where? Did they help or hurt the situation?

A: I checked into the battered women's shelter. I didn't want to involve my parents because my dad was already saying things like he'd kill my Ex and didn't care about going to jail. The Battered women's shelter helped keep me from being homeless and hungry but didn't help very much with seeking gainful employment. The time to check into the shelter was too sporadic and too unaccommodating to go to interviews and/or work at all during the day. It seemed to be counter-productive in every way in that regards. I felt like we all needed some sort of counseling as well while we were in this place, but we didn't receive any help. My roommate was so dysfunctional that she would beat and scream at her teenage kid every day, even when he wasn't doing anything wrong. She blamed her son for her husband's abuse since her husband disapproved of her son's sexuality. So the shelter helped, but didn't help.

Even though Vickie mentioned challenges with the shelter check-in times, she reconnected with Jesus, her true bail bondsman, while there. She landed gainful employment and is now flourishing in her career and community. Let the safe house or shelter be what you need. Safety and security for you and your children to regroup, recover, and restart. These boundaries are in place to protect you as a victim of domestic violence and abuse in your early recovery phase from yourself. Oftentimes victims do not realize how much they have become conditioned by the condition they were living in. They tend to attract and even seek out relationships that are similar to what they just left out of. Your mind, both conscious and subconscious and your emotions need to go through a detoxification and transformation.

Ellen's Story

Q: Why do women ignore the initial signs of abuse?

A: I remember it like it was 3 days ago. The very first sign was when we were discussing our lives before marriage, he spoke about how he was living with another woman and I mentioned that I was with a guy. He suddenly smacked me in my mouth so hard. We then fought like we were in the WWF and I fought back. He told me that I had crossed the line. Yet, he wanted to make up and even have sex. I couldn't do it. He went to work with a black eye. Afterwards there was more emotional abuse. He would have flash backs of his previous marriage and he just snapped all the time. As time went on I rededicated my life to the Lord and he progressively got more and more depressed. Later in the marriage, I found out that it was his mother that told him that he needed to beat me because she was abused. She later apologized after I had left him and she had given her life to the Lord. He progressively became an alcoholic searching for his identity. He got violent and I ran to a neighbor and they refused to call the police because they didn't want to get involved so I had to run to another neighbors' house and they called the police. There were no signs because he was always so calm and suddenly he hit me while we were sitting on the couch. After that moment of truth, he blamed me for everything, even for things the first wife did. This was approximately six years into the marriage. Whatever his mother told him was law. But let's talk about my Mom. My mom advised me to stick it out because "he's just going through a spell." It seemed like every August through October he would get worse. I would tell my *mom, I'm getting out of this* and she would say, "No. You don't need to go anywhere. Just stick it out." A counselor told me to tell my mom to stay out of it and for me to get out of it. I had to say, "*I'm not going back mom and this discussion is closed.*"

Q: What excuses did YOU use to stay?
A: Actually I had three reasons why I stayed
1. I had children and I didn't make enough to leave and live in a decent area so I would tough it out until our break came.
2. I couldn't see myself divorced because I didn't think I was ready to fight that kind of fight even when someone told me that he would have to pay me child support.
3. Although I said that I was staying for the sake of the kids, I was actually staying because I was gripped by fear of what might or might not happen.

Q: What was your breaking point?
A: After the fight that got the neighbors involved, I told him he needed counseling. We went 3 times and it ended.

But things went backwards. I then began to focus on myself, the church, the kids, and ignored him. However, when we got home we would feel the darkness and as we stepped in the house there were accusations and arguing. I mentally blocked him out. The only way I could deal with it was to get more into the Lord. I would tell the kids that he had a free will and all we can do is pray for him and for his mind. I began to look into how other relatives within his family were acting and noticed a pattern of depression and mental illness. Eventually it came out that even he was bipolar. He started calling people and leaving threatening messages. I was warned that he had a spirit of murder on him. Even then I had not made my mind up to leave. At the 23 year mark of marriage, one day I wrote him a letter saying to him that we were not getting along and that we needed counseling in order to move forward. I found the letter ripped up and thrown in the trash. That was when I knew I had to move! I didn't want my daughters to grow up thinking this is how life is supposed to be in marriage. I would try to tell them that he was sick and that they needed to pray for him. They became angry at me for allowing it. He constantly would tell me to get out and that I wasn't contributing but he had 3 credit cards in my name. I was in debt and didn't know it. Nevertheless, we still didn't leave then because I couldn't afford $800 rent and when I went to get help I was told I had to get rid of my car in order to have lower income to get help. It was ridiculous! I kept the kids busy and we learned how to live in the dysfunction by staying away and in church. Then it came to one last fight. This time the girls got involved and that was the breaking point. They jumped in to save me and I knew it was time for me to save us all. At that point, I sought God for a plan and stuck with the plan.

Q: What scriptures, if any did you rely on during and after the relationship ended.
A: My favorite scripture was and still is Isaiah 54:17 NLT "But in that coming day no weapon turned against you will succeed. You will silence every voice raised up to accuse you. These benefits are enjoyed by the servants of the Lord; their vindication will come from me. I, the Lord, have spoken!" Ellen stated that she had this scripture posted on her dashboard, the mirror, everywhere! Her daughters will tell you, whenever they got in the car that is what they pleaded, decreed and declared.

Q: Did you call in reinforcements to help you? If so, who? Did they help or hurt the situation?
A: Yes, I knew people would want to help but the down fall was the place that I would have to go wouldn't be a good environment for the kids to live. Once we did move, someone gave me a deposit, co-workers gave me furniture, and others gave me money. The place that we went was so peaceful and the Lord gave me a confirmation that it was going to be okay and that I could do this.

Q: Do you feel it was the right decision to stay at the time?
A: Yes, I do. I didn't want to have to raise them in that part of town being single with young girls. There were so many things hitting me, I just didn't want to fight with it at that time. Too much was going on with the kids emotionally, adding the thought of the neighborhood

conditions was overwhelming. I felt and believed that I wasn't adequate enough to handle it.

Looking back, if I could give advice to a person who is in the same or similar situation I would say, "*You are stronger than you think you are. Things are not going to be as bad as you think they are going to be.*" People stepped in and others worked with me when they found out that I was in an abusive situation. I'm sure it would have happened when the girls were smaller but I was too afraid to find that out. Now, there are resources and organizations that can help you because in the long run your children will be damaged mentally and emotionally. After we left, my daughters needed help because they didn't believe they could do anything. They were still in a cage even if they were not in the house any longer. They would hear his voice telling them, "You can't do that!" It took some time to get them out of that cage but they are now soaring. Reach out! Reach out to any and every person and organization that you can to get out of that situation NOW because you don't have to stay. I was afraid, but I know now that if you connect with someone who understands and has been through it you can come out of this. Today there are grants and programs available to assist you with housing. Just look into it. Speak Out and Step Out!

Tears are streaming as I speak of this event in my life even after I've been divorced for several years because it was a sad story. Yet, I'm not depressed. These are tears of relief, release, and VICTORY! Because God began to open doors for multiple streams of income using the skills I already had.

Say this with me, *"I, just like Jesus, [daily] walk in favor, stature, and wisdom with God and all the people."* Luke 2:52 NLT

It makes me angry that he did that to me. He destroyed my credit! I had to pay for that as part of the divorce decree because it was in my name. How does a person do that when you are supposed to be a team? I don't really know why I am angry. I guess it's because I am still unable to buy or get certain things because my credit is jacked up. Nevertheless I do what I want to do, I go where I want to go and I have what the Lord has for me. Today I had to breathe the Lord In and invite Him in to the place that I didn't realize was there. That place of resentment and bitterness. Today I forgive fully and move forward. Thank you Father for this opportunity to snap back into my position in the Spirit and move forward in my calling, into a place of wholeness and to help someone else survive. I feel like getting in my car and going somewhere!

Hallelujah! Ellen started singing a song, "Now I'm Free! I'm Free at Last! Free to live the life I want and forget about my past. NOW, I'm Free! I'm free at last! Free to hope. Free to dream. Free to love at last."

Julie's Story

I met Julie at the nail salon. When I told her about my book she was amazed and shared her personal experience with me. Julie shared with me that she could remember it as if it was yesterday. She was about 25 years old when she moved in with a guy who had a severe asthma health issue and already had children. The young man would have terrible asthma attacks that caused him to be hospitalized. This caused Julie to become closer to the guy's mother and children than she did to him. She thought that his near death experiences would cause him to change but it never did. Julie recalled how they would have horrible arguments, break up and she would leave him off and on. When she was away from him she felt so good about herself and she felt SO free. Yet, overwhelmed by the guilt of hurting or disappointing his mother and his children, in addition to the fact that this man was so sickly Julie went back to him and returned to low self-esteem, low self-worth and more verbal abuse and treatment. Things got so bad. One day Julie decided she was going to leave for good. She told her lover she was leaving. He grabbed her by her throat, began choking her and told her that she would never leave him alive.

Q: Why do you think women tell an abuser that they are leaving them instead of simply walking away or running for their lives?
A: Julie could not answer this question. She said, "I guess I wanted to give him one last chance to change but when he started choking me, I knew it was over."

Julie told me that although she was shaken, she still made up in her mind that somehow she would leave him. One week after her decision to leave he died of an asthma attack. Julie stated that she moved on with her life, is now happily married and has a new baby girl. When asked what initial signs of abuse she overlooked, Julie suggests, people should pay attention to what a person is saying to them and believe them. Don't make assumptions. Julie advises that people take more time to get to know someone before getting involved with them. I asked Julie if she thinks she would have actually left the guy if he had not died and she responded with an emphatic "Absolutely!" She asserted that she had a plan and was going to follow the plan no matter what. Julie said that she realized after being choked by him that his sickly lifestyle and family ties no longer overrode the value of her life and freedom. Julie said that she never told her family about what she was going through because she thought her family would feel indifferent towards her because of the life she was living when in fact it wasn't that way at all. They were relieved that she got away from this abusive situation.

Leah's Story

I didn't see things as an abusive relationship because of what I had defined in my mind to be considered abuse. To me abuse was what I witnessed my cousin go through. She was dragged into the street and received threats of murder. However, my situation was more emotionally abusive because I did not feel good about myself when I was with the person that I married.

In theory, the guy that I was with met the check boxes for being a good boyfriend and spouse. Comparing him to the last husband, who was a sex addict and adulterer and comparing him to my childhood coming from a broken home, I thought as long as the person seemed committed and devoted to me it was okay to accept or tolerate some of the other things he was doing to me. Initially he negated my work, my personal aspirations, and even my emotional availability. He treated me as though my input was not valued on decision making. Yet, after two years of dating this person and being treated this way I married him.

Q: Why did you stay and even get married and how did it progress in marriage?
A: It was the apology that would win me back. He would say it was all a misunderstanding and I wanted to hear him say he was okay with me. However, if I did something that he felt was unacceptable, he would "punish me" emotionally by not being available, not answering the phone, making decisions about career changes, and started putting his friends input over mine. He would ignore me completely. He would say that he didn't want to deal with me. We would go to counseling and discuss our issues. He would tell the counselor how he felt as a form of confession, yet not apply any of the counselor's recommended solutions and strategies.

One night we went out and he was angry about everything including his outfit. We were late and he started drinking. By drink number eight I asked him to slow down and he continued drinking and started calling me names in front of people that I didn't know. He started getting aggressive with me because I was ignoring him out of shear embarrassment. It was so bad that another couple tried to help me. I had called an Uber ride to come get me but watching him cry in the street made me feel sorry for him so I cancelled the ride and drove us both home. Giving serious thought over this event I thought this wasn't going to be a good relationship to grow old in because he had so much animosity built up against me and would pour it out publicly. I thought maybe we could work it out if I became more of a stereotypical wife by downplaying myself more. Then maybe we could work things out. So we went back to counseling. He confessed to the counselor again yet when I changed my career or had dinner ready, he would not come home. He would tell me that he would not change his schedule for me. Later he started assuming I was cheating on him and started going through my iPad and reading my emails and text messages. He would see that I was sharing what was happening between us with my Mom. He got extremely angry which scared me. The violation of my privacy was my breaking point because I had not given him any reason not to trust me. I felt like he was searching for something wrong with me. Feeling like I was being spied on in my own home was the last straw. A week later, he left me and the relationship ended. I realized that he wasn't going to be happy with me because I was not the ideal wife in his mind. For me, I felt like I was a good person and a good wife but why wasn't it working? I just wanted that validation from him that I was all those things and I wanted to feel…*Sigh*! Hey, externally I was seen as a good friend, hard worker and validated but I wanted that same comfort and validation at home. Instead I was treated like the competition. Speculating; our backgrounds were so different that it could have been a key source of conflict because the women didn't work or have a say in any decision making in his family. Whereas my family did not have men involved in my home, women made most or all of the decisions. After the divorce, I was told by some of my friends that I didn't put enough into the relationship because the man is supreme. That wasn't my belief. However, I did believe in respect and honor which I gave continually.

Q: Did you seek help from scripture?

A: When I would read the bible regarding divorce or a woman's place in the home they really didn't help me to deal with the mistreatment but I did make more efforts to stay because I know how God felt about divorce and I wanted my marriage to work. After it got so bad, I sought God's grace, mercy, healing, and forgiveness. That caused me to follow God's Word. I started attending church more and seeking to be God's child again. I trusted that I could find my way back to God's grace.

Q: You mentioned that you wanted to hear him say he was okay with you and the way you were. What contributed to that need?

A: It's a partnership so I thought that he was the best person in every aspect and I wanted him to feel the same about me. Everyone who gets married wants their opinion respected and to have a sense of security. The big event of the wedding brought some sense of stability but the rest of his actions didn't. My father left when I was three years old and I changed schools 14 times, between kindergarten and the 12th grade. Even as an adult I graduated from college a year ahead of my friends so we didn't even get to start life together, plus I moved from place to place. I was searching for stability and security in relationships and in my life; "Until death do us part." It was a disappointment when I realized I was with my spouse and I wasn't his best friend. He didn't have my back. Even though I was married to someone I didn't have that sense of stability and safety. I just felt like it was danger and distrust.

Q: Since the divorce, what is your source of stability and security today?

A: I felt as a Christian I failed when my marriage didn't work out. The personal marriage boot camp that consisted of prayers, scriptures, music, and coaching with Apostle Tina McCrea helped me rebuild my relationship with God. I learned that I was not abandoned by Jesus. Gaining strength to talk about it has helped me to grow stronger and abolish shame. Through that sharing I have received support from friends and family that has gotten me through it all.

Q: How did you grow and what did you learn from that relationship?

A: One thing that I discovered during prayer was that I was struggling with being alone. The marriage boot camp uncovered that it was a spirit of abandonment. The source of that feeling actually came from instability, constantly moving, growing up as an only child and the lack of interaction with my dad. My grandfather was more like a dad to me so I didn't know that a dad was supposed to be around all the time.

Q: Do you feel empowered to Break Free, Stay Free, Be Free?

A: I do. I followed my mother all over the place as a child. I used to fear being alone. Spiraling down, people would frequently come and go in and out of my life. I searched hard to find a partner in marriage for stability. There was a recurring dream that I would have that depicted me free falling as though I needed to catch myself. It would wake me up out of my sleep. Since the divorce, the dream has stopped. I feel more comfortable and stable because I've discovered that I am never alone. Jesus was there with me all the way. I've made a commitment to myself by purchasing my own home. I'm calm and confident in who I am after reconnecting with who Jesus is to me and who I am through Him. I feel so humbled that a person who looks like a dot in the universe, God orchestrated bringing the right people together to pull me into His Grace and into my healing. Reading the bible there are other people who have gone through things like you but they found victory just as I did. I am who I am and I do not need to hide a piece of me to make someone feel better about themselves. I believe I am a good person with or without someone. You can be too through Christ Jesus!

Faith's Story

Here's a story from a young lady we will call Faith. She is a teenager who experienced abuse resulting from seeking love and acceptance in a relationship she wasn't ready for. Faith's story begins when she started attending a summer camp one year. She was twelve at the time, just about to go into the 6th grade. She met a guy who was tall, looked smart and seemed mature. At first Faith says he was nice, charming and caring. Being younger and seeking acceptance from peers it was great when everyone wanted to be her friend because of this guy, who was popular. Then everything went bad. He became more possessive by treating her like she was his property. If she spoke with guys who were not his friends he would grab her wrist and drag her away angrily saying, "I told you that you do not talk to anybody that I do not introduce you to." Faith said she would apologize and comply because she would recall stories her mother told her about when she was abused and she was afraid that it would happen to her. Eventually the boy began to require Faith to allow him to perform sexual acts on her in private as well as in public. This made Faith feel humiliated and degraded. She told one of her friends she met at the summer camp that she wanted to kill herself if she could not get away from the camp. The very next day she walks into the summer camp the counselor says to her, "Oh, I thought you were going to kill yourself. At least that's what I heard." That statement made Faith feel like nobody would take her seriously about her thoughts of harming herself. Faith began to think about how her parents would feel if she did take her life. She felt abandoned by her parents having to work and leave her at that camp so she had to say to herself, suck it up, and get over it. Trying to move on, Faith asked the counselor if the boy was there and he said, yes. She sees the boy as he's running up on her. She's thinking *he's going to tear me up*. Instead he embraced her saying he heard she was going to kill herself. Confused, Faith starting thinking it must have been her fault that he was hurting her so she decided to not talk back and try to make him happier. It was like a kiss and make-up kind of thing.

The very NEXT day, it seemed like things got worse as if the situation that happened the day before never took place, as if it was washed away. He started taking her food away knowing she could not eat the camp food and gave it to his friends. She was required to bring more snacks and food each day for him and his friends. The tipping point was when it was adventure day and the kids were all playing with water. It was all fun and games. The counselors were a part of it. Faith was becoming hungered due to the fact the boy had taken her lunch and she was fighting depression. As they all were playing, water got on Faith's bathing suit and the boy wanted to start touching her. He got angry and encouraged his friends who were much older than them to throw more water on her. She began to run away from them but slipped and fell. Faith said she hated herself for that. The friends grabbed her legs and her arms and they started swinging her back and forth like a hammock. He got some of his friends to get a large orange cooler like they use at football games and dumped it in her face. She felt like she was about to drown. She wasn't sure if she was having a panic attack or not. The counselor was watching all along. Finally, they dropped her and dumped the rest of the water on her and walked away. Faith said she felt so dirty. There was no recovery time in between the dunks. Nobody asked how she was. Nobody thought it was a problem because observers had become used to watching Faith doing and being whatever he wanted her to be. Immediately following that incident Faith, dazed and dehydrated asked the counselor if she could go get water. The boy came to Faith dirty and demanded her to remove her swimsuit top and began to suck on her breasts. A life guard spotted them and the boy ran off. The life guard and Faith's eyes connected as she lifted up her top. The life guard later approached Faith informing her that he saw what happened. She said that she tried to tell him that it wasn't what it looked like but he didn't quite believe her. He advised her by saying; "just stay away from him and be careful" but he never reported what he saw to anyone. When I asked Faith what was her turning point she said it wasn't her walking away because she was fed up but it was when she returned to camp from a family vacation and found out that the boy had "cheated" on her with a close friend who she considered as a sister. She didn't know whether or not to feel happy or betrayed. She said his friends ridiculed her for not "fighting for" her relationship. The girls that knew the guy knew exactly why she was acting that way. Faith felt better about herself but she still wanted to be a friend and around him just to prove him wrong. When I asked her what was wrong about what she said, she replied "I Don't know, it was like that feeling when you've been down played all that time then you finally get to show your real colors so you stay around them just to treat them like you've wanted to be treated the entire time." She described it like you want to stick up for yourself and be abrasive to the point where it's like sandpaper on skin. Of course he tried punching her in the arm as if she was one of the guys. Faith gave him a warning that she would fight back. His friends chuckled and he hit her again and she hit back even harder. They did not speak to each other again until the last day of the summer camp. Faith said he began to apologize for all that happened and began to kiss her. She pushed him away but didn't tell him that it was unacceptable. She said she should have spoken up but she didn't. Faith was never okay with how the situation ended. Even as she rode past that place it was like torture. Because it was such shame associated with that place she had to turn her head whenever she would go by there. She was ashamed at the fact her parents didn't know. Faith waited for years before she told her parents about what happened because she was afraid of the consequences as well as the fact that the boy's mother was a police officer so she thought justice would not come to him. When she did tell her parents they had so many questions. "Why didn't you tell us?" She knew they would want to get justice and she didn't want to open that wound again. Faith said that she had to forgive herself for not taking the responsibility of speak up and saying no. When I asked if she had forgiven the person, she said that an inch of her forgives him but she felt so damaged that it was hard to fully forgive. It has made her so paranoid in relationships because she compares people to that abusive relationship. It made her resent her parents for leaving her there yet she could not tell them what the source of her frustration stemmed from. When asked whether or not she was much better person since that incident? Faith replied, "I'm working on being a better me. I will not tolerate sexual abuse, harassment or anything of that nature in my life again. Even talking about it now makes me realize that I have deep corners in my heart where I have to heal. Areas of abandonment, pain, hurt, feeling devalued. Nevertheless, it's a journey that I am on and I can surely say that I am blossoming. That's why I chose the name

Faith for this story, because I have Faith that I will be the person that I fully want to become." Faith ended her story by saying, "I know this story is a doozy but I hope it helps someone; especially young people. Do not lessen yourself for another person no matter how sweet or how charming they may seem. It's not worth devaluing yourself in order to make another person feel valued. Your happiness with yourself is way more important. Believe me! Talk to someone. Talk to your parents or someone close. Let them guide you. Talk to a therapist as I did. Ultimately, you can talk to God I guess."

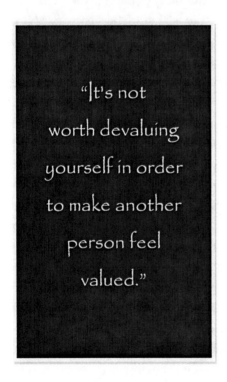

"It's not worth devaluing yourself in order to make another person feel valued."

This is so touching. Faith is still on her journey towards healing but she's moving forward. If you are a young person or even an older person like faith and you are comparing people to the abusive person each time you meet someone new by saying, "Well, they are not as bad as XYZ." I urge you as I urged Faith today to remove the bad relationship from your comparison scale. Start with a clean slate of FAITH in God. It may be hard for you to even trust God because you don't understand why He allowed it to happen to you. Faith never knew her story would be in this book, blessing you today. Please consider this. Build your expectations on the promises of God not on TV relationships. Trust God to present you with a person that is a gift from him in a relationship according to Proverbs 18:22 AMP "He who finds a [true] wife finds a good thing and obtains favor from the Lord." This takes listening to and obeying the voice of God's Holy Spirit who will place the right desire in your heart. This takes Faith!

Could this be YOU? Are you stuck in an abusive relationship because you actually feel sorry for your abuser? What about your life? What other way can you empower both yourself and the other person break free, stay free and BE free? Some people have a need to be needed which can become a dangerous obsession if the Lord is not invited into that place in their lives. I suggest you pray and ask the Lord to deliver you from a need to be needed. You were not born to be degraded, put down, beaten, and abused. You are not another person's Savior. Jesus is the Only Savior of mankind! The fact is, Jesus died on the cross for the forgiveness of sin because you are valuable to God. God needs you as a part of His Kingdom. He will place you in an environment where you are valued, affirmed, loved, and cherished. You must believe this about yourself my friend! You do not need to announce you are leaving! Don't try to use your threats of leaving as a weapon. This is very dangerous. Remember what happened to Julie? Statistics show many women have died attempting to leave this way so you must *use wisdom*!

71

According to the Domestic Abuse Center of the Florida Keys:

On average, a woman will leave an abusive relationship seven times before she leaves for good.

Approximately 75% of women who are killed by their batterers are murdered when they attempt to leave or after they have left an abusive relationship.

Before you panic, these stats are not intended to scare you. They are here to help you become empowered in your decision making. Be sure to share your plans with a supporter not the abuser. Once you've established a plan, stick to the plan and execute the plan with wisdom.

CHAPTER 7
HEALING FOR SURVIVORS

There were others that I requested an interview with but the scab of the abusive experience was too soft for them to talk about it. I say this because it was too painful to remember and I truly understand. Even as others discussed their experiences or as I wrote about my own for this book, the memories were as though it were 3 days ago or yesterday for some. Yet, after they removed the scab, the open wound was exposed to the healing balm of Jesus Christ. The oil of Holy Spirit poured into that place and we were able to walk away from one another with joy and celebration for deliverance.

If you are a survivor but you are going through what I described, there is also healing available for you. Invite the Lord Jesus Christ into that place of anger, resentment, bitterness, and hurt. My current husband and I attended a Forward training at Victory World Church in Norcross, Georgia. They taught us that Forgiveness is a key part in Moving Forward in our relationship with God and with others. I met a lady who is in such bondage to unforgiveness and resentment that she has become a hostage in her home and what happened to her consumes every conversation. Unforgiveness affects our health, prayer life, relationships, everything. Forgiving does not require that you deny what happened was real. What most of us have done is repressed or buried the hurt which also causes sin of bitterness and resentment. Others of us do what we just spoke about and read testimonies about, and that is make excuses; "They didn't mean it. That's just how they are or a spell they are going through right now." Even if the person never changes, you need to forgive. This does not mean that you are guaranteed to reconcile with the abuser. Reconciliation must first start with the Spirit of Truth. Sometimes people who hurt people are unwilling to admit they are wrong. The man that murdered my aunt went to his grave and would not say he was sorry to my cousin who was present at every parole hearing. Forgiveness is not dependent upon another person's actions. It is a requirement by God for you and me. Matt.16:14-15 NLT "If you forgive those who sin against you, your Heavenly Father will forgive you. But if you refuse to forgive others, your Father will not forgive your sins." I realize this is a process. It may not be a one-time event for you, so I want to close this book with a prayer that I hope helps you.

TINA R. McCREA

CHAPTER 8
MY HEALING JOURNEY TO MY
NEW HUSBAND

After breaking free, the first step in my personal healing process was to seek counseling. As I mentioned in Chapter 3, take advantage of your Employee Assistance Program, if you have one. It's confidential and it's usually a benefit that we often overlook. I requested a Christian counselor or at least someone that knew God as Jehovah. The closest they got for me was a person who was of the Jewish faith. He asked me great questions regarding my faith. Looking back on it, I believe sharing with him was a witnessing opportunity.

This counselor helped me to understand boundaries that I didn't realize were lacking in my life. Together, we explored how I got into the situation in the first place. I made discoveries about how and why I overlooked what was being said to me. I learned how to set and stand by boundaries that included honor and respect. In addition, I learned that I got here because I was looking for love in a fatherly role, someone to replace the gap that existed from my dad. My dad and I had the best relationship before he passed. All needed to do was trust God because He already had a plan in place to mend that gap. My dad and I had the best relationship before he passed. Trusting God can save us so much time and pain.

Following counseling, establish healthy boundaries for yourself. Be able to say, "That's not the appropriate way to speak to me" and "I don't like it when you use that tone or language with me." My eyes were open to how to identify unhealthy boundaries. I learned to say, "That's not the best relationship for me."

I felt so free and liberated when I established those boundaries. It didn't matter who crossed the line. It could have been a pastor, a church member, a co-worker or even a manager. I set healthy boundaries by saying no and not feeling guilty. I learned that 'no', was an anointed word, even if I was a Christian.

Once I got out of that abusive relationship, my new manager would call me every Friday evening and curse me out like he was drunk or something. The profanity left me speechless and shaking. One day I said, "Enough is enough!" He required me to meet him for a business meeting. On our drive to dinner, I told him how uncomfortable it made me feel when he spoke to me that way. I explained how difficult it was to provide him with the answers he needed because I was trying to process why he was cursing and screaming. His reply was, "You should always have a certain level of fear for your boss." Bells went off on the inside of me and red flags started waving. I said to myself, "I will not walk in fear!" Let's just say after a 'come to Jesus meeting' with human resources, he welcomed me with open arms and respect. That spirit was put in its place because proper boundaries were set.

Some people who survive domestic violence or abusive relationships may say they will never get married or even have a serious relationship again. However, when asked if I would ever marry again, I always said that I would and the person that I married would be a pastor and love God more than he loved me. Well, that man came along in 1995. Gary McCrea. I thought he was the loudest, country, most obnoxious and lame person I had ever met. In fact, my ex-husband used to make fun of him. Brother Gary, as everyone called him at the time, was a member of the church I used to attend when I was going through the terrible marriage. He had even been out to our house for a cookout with some friends. After I divorced, Gary used to stand in the church lobby right outside the bookstore where I worked and announce to anyone passing by that the Lord was going to bless him with a wife and how happy he was going to be. He would announce when he was going to Bishop T.D. Jakes' Manpower events and say that he would return with a wife. I would be in the bookstore dusting off and restocking shelves with my lip turned up saying, "Lord, please bless him with a wife so he can SHUT UP!"

Since we had mutual friends, we often ended up at the same events. He was so loud but seemed like a soft person. He wasn't the bad boy type that I liked. He began to drop hints but I wasn't quite getting them. He baked cakes for my birthday and gave me special gifts. I would say thank you and keep going. Honey, I would freeze that cake and slice off of it like single folks do. The man could cook! I wasn't in to him though. He even offered to help with the youth ministry I oversaw.

Someone asked me what I thought about Gary since he was single. I was like 'Heck no!" He didn't seem like my type. I didn't know anything but rough and abusive bad boys. Well, Gary was persistent. Somehow he managed to need a ride to an event and I drove him. He started talking about how when he got married he would be the kind of man that would support a wife that was in ministry and not be intimidated by her spiritual gifts, even if she was in a higher position in ministry. He said he would even be willing to help take care of the children if she had to do ministry. I had the music blasting in the car and wasn't really paying him any attention. The more he said, the more I tuned in. I turned down the music and asked him to repeat himself. He did and smiled. I didn't say anything; I just took it in.

Finally, my biological brother who was my roommate at the time, told me that he thought "Brother Gary" liked me. I told my brother I didn't think so but my brother said Gary was too nice to me. "He's nice to everybody," I replied. I told my brother I would pray about it.

On July 19, 1998, Gary asked me to join him after church for lunch at Red Lobster. I rushed to tell ask a male minister what should I do? The friend told me to ask Gary a direct question, "What are your intentions toward me?" If he flinches, he's not the one, the friend said. If he looks you in the eye and gives you a straight answer, then he might be the one. Excited, and thinking I was going to expose Brother Gary for being no good, I accepted the invitation.

With a big smile, Gary escorted me to my seat at the restaurant and we ordered our salads. I couldn't wait to spring the big question on him. He blessed the food and as soon as he took his first bite, I said, "I have a question for you." He softly responded, "Go ahead ask." You could hear the tone of suspicion in my voice when I said, "What are your intentions towards me?" I smirked and stared him down with that 'um hum' look. He put his fork down, looked me in the eye and with determination said, "Well, I've been fasting and praying for some time and I believe that by this time next year, you will be my wife." My blood pressure shot up! I was screaming on the inside, 'What!?!' Then I fell over on the booth seat. I don't know how long I was down there. I'm looking under the table and saying to myself, "Oh no!" My friend didn't tell me what to say if he said that. Could Gary be "The One?" As I gained my composure and set up, "Brother Gary" was staring me down and waiting for a response. With my mouth open and barely breathing, I finally said, "Well, I guess you are all right and I kinda like you." I told him I would have to fast and pray myself to see what the Lord had to say. He agreed to fast with me. On my drive home, I asked God, "Could this be? I am enjoying being single, Lord. You are going to have to speak so clearly to me because he doesn't even seem like my type, Lord."

The Lord began to show me that my heart's desire had changed as I continued to make Jesus my delight. Everything had changed. Our dates consisted of me asking him so many questions that he said he felt like he had been interrogated by the FBI. I even asked about his family lineage. "Who was your grandfather? Did he beat your grandmother? Who is your Father? Why don't you mention him much? Was your Father abusive?" The questions went on and on for months until one day Gary purchased a book called, *Before You Say "I Do"* by H. Norman Wright and Wes Roberts. Each date consisted of walking through a chapter of that book before we went anywhere or did activities. I learned that the dating/courtship time needs to be spent communicating and interacting with others in your circle instead of staring at a movie screen for hours and learning nothing about the person who claims they love you and you say you love. Honestly, this was a very painful process at times. The closer we seemed to get the more fear caused me to pushed Gary away. I didn't even realize that fear was there. Sometimes our dates ended after reading a chapter because I would be crying uncontrollably. I felt like a person who had been peacefully sleeping only to wake up to their front door unlocked and wide open. I realized that there were wounds that were still open. Some days I would make Gary cry out, "What did he do to you!?! I am not that man!"

It took pre-marital counseling, fasting, praying, and months for me to realize that Gary was not that man. When I asked, "Why do you want to marry me?" his response was, "Why not you? Why don't you deserve to be happy, to be loved?" With one last push, I told him that I couldn't be the one for him because I could not have any children. I had been barren in my previous marriage. Gary's reply was, "That's not what God's word says about your life. It says that you shall have whatever you ask for when you pray, if you believe it." He told me that he had faith to believe that God would give me a child. And even if He didn't, I had plenty of children that I ministered to in the youth ministry. Those could be my children. He would not budge. I began to love him more and more because of his faith, the peace, and joy I experienced when I was with him. I thank God for that.

When I was praying and trying to figure out this newfound peace, I came across this scripture: Colossians 3:15AMP - *And let the peace (soul harmony which comes) from Christ rule (act as umpire continually) in your hearts [deciding and settling with finality all questions that arise in your minds, in that peaceful state] to which as [members of Christ's] one body you were also called [to live]. And be thankful (appreciative), [giving praise to God always].* The peace from Holy Spirit let me know that this relationship was safe.

Gary honored me and never tried to make weird advances. I thought it wasn't normal because men did it all the time. Even the married men at church started making advances towards me once I was divorced. It was scary! The fact that he didn't made me feel weird. I had to check my mindset. Being treated with honor and respect felt odd. I hear woman say that to me often and I have to remind them that honor and respect is God's normal.

When I returned to my minister friend who taught me the flinch test to ask when do you know it's time to move forward in a new relationship, he said, "If you are ready and able to be vulnerable in that same place like it was the first time you've ever dated, then you know that you are healed from past hurts."

Gary and I experienced such a new beginning on September 4, 1999, when we said, I do… until death do us part. Just as I hoped for, God blessed me with a husband that loves Him more than he does me and loves me like Christ loves the church. And just as I hoped for, this man is serving with me in ministry and as promised, he's not intimidated by my spiritual gifts or my position in the market place. On top of all of that, Gary and I used to pray about a dream I had of a daughter named Gina, a combination of the G from Gary and INA from Tina. On November 25, 2000, we had a beautiful baby girl whom we named Gina. God truly does heal the broken hearted and binds up *every* wound. I had a cousin tell me once, "You can live with a scar but an open wound will kill you." I pray this story helps you heal today.

CHAPTER 9
CLOSING PRAYER

Father, I thank you for bringing me out of that abusive relationship. Lord, every time I think of _____ and what they took me through I feel that pain as if it was yesterday. I still can't help but wonder and question why they did that to ME Lord! Father, I even wondered at times why you allowed them to do it. Lord, I thought all of this pain was gone but when I pause and think of it for any length of time, I realized it is still there. Lord Jesus, I invite you into that place of pain and ask you to demolish every stronghold that I have erected. Bind me to your healing and peace. Lord, make me really and unquestionably free by your liberating power today. Jesus, I make a conscious decision to follow your example and I say, "Father, forgive them, for they did not know what they were doing because they were operating out of their own pain and the control of a spirit that was trying to destroy both of us." Lord, I give you glory for sparing my life to have my own story to tell. Thank you Father for a renewed mind, renewed heart, and for a fresh start. In the mighty name of Jesus Christ who came in the flesh. AMEN!

ABOUT THE AUTHOR

Tina R. McCrea is an ordained minister and apostle of Christ our Lord. She and her husband, Apostle Gary L. McCrea, are co-founders and co-pastors of the Greater Atlanta-based Without a Trace Ministries Inc., which is adopted from John 8:36 AMP - *"So if the Son liberates you [makes you free], then you are really and unquestionably free."* The ministry is dedicated to helping families become free through the power of Christ.

A Louisville, KY, native, Tina is a passionate leader and a woman who is serious about advancing God's Kingdom. She has served as a Christian Educator for children's church, Sunday School, women and couples. She served as an anointed youth director and book store manager in a thriving ministry in Atlanta.

As a domestic violence survivor, Tina is dedicated to helping other women and men shatter this stronghold in their lives. Her ministry gifts include chaplaincy/visitation ministry; individual and group outreach; adult and couples Bible instructor; and women's ministry coordinator. She has facilitated workshops and masterminds with titles such as Becoming a Contagious Christian; Focus or Failure; God's Armor Bearers; Put Your Dreams to the Test, Modeling Christ In The DIP, Climbing the Corporate Ladder in High Heels; and FamilyLife Ministries' HomeBuilders Couples Bible Study.

With more than 35 years of experience in project management, process improvement, and as an O&S professional, her focus is on marketplace evangelism, leadership development, and cultivating the whole family.

Tina completed the Lay Theology Institute at Emory's Candler School of Theology, is a graduate of Billy Graham School of Evangelism, and has received other leadership training in the area of Pastoral Care & Counseling and Ethical Leadership. She also studied leadership at Beulah Heights University. Tina is also a certified project manager through Project Management Leadership Group, certified LEAN 1B through OEE, and certified John Maxwell coach, speaker, and trainer.

Tina, her husband and their daughter, Gina, reside in Stone Mountain, Ga.

FOR MORE TITLES
FROM EX3 BOOKS

VISIT OUR WEBSITE AT:
www.EX3Books.com

Feel free to share your reviews of
Empowering Truth
via our website, email info@EX3Books.com,
or on Amazon.com.

CPSIA information can be obtained
at www.ICGtesting.com
Printed in the USA
LVOW08s0032091116
512211LV00007B/73/P